BANANA PALACE

ALSO BY DANA LEVIN

Sky Burial
Wedding Day
In the Surgical Theatre

DANA LEVIN

BANANA PALACE

For Patrick,
Fellow Traveller!
with gratitude for your
light, in this rich +
treacherous world,
Dana
Oct 2016

COPPER CANYON PRESS

PORT TOWNSEND, WASHINGTON

Cover art: *Fractal Galaxy* by Silver Sky

Copper Canyon Press is in residence at Fort Worden State Park in Port Townsend, Washington, under the auspices of Centrum. Centrum is a gathering place for artists and creative thinkers from around the world, students of all ages and backgrounds, and audiences seeking extraordinary cultural enrichment.

LIBRARY OF CONGRESS CATALOGING-IN-PUBLICATION DATA

Name: Levin, Dana, author.
Title: Banana palace / Dana Levin.
Description: Port Townsend, WA : Copper Canyon Press, [2016]
Identifiers: LCCN 2016011750 | ISBN 9781556595059 (softcover : acid-free paper)
Subjects: | BISAC: POETRY / American / General.
Classification: LCC PS3562.E88953 A6 2016 | DDC 811/.54—dc23
LC record available at https://lccn.loc.gov/2016011750

98765432 FIRST PRINTING

Copper Canyon Press
Post Office Box 271
Port Townsend, Washington 98368
www.coppercanyonpress.org

ACKNOWLEDGMENTS

Thanks to the editors of the following publications, for offering these poems early homes:

AGNI: Lady Xoc

The American Poetry Review: Across the Sea

American Poets: A Debris Field of Apocalypticians—a Murder of Crows

Argos Poetry Calendar, 2015: Fortune Cookie

Berfrois: Murray, My (reprint)

The Best American Poetry 2015 (Sherman Alexie, guest editor): Watching the Sea Go (reprint)

Blackbird: Moo and Thrall (1st printing)

Black Warrior Review: Meanwhile

Boston Review: Murray, My (1st printing)

Devouring the Green: Fear of a Human Planet: Dmitry Itskov: A Cento

New England Review: The Point of the Needle

The New York Times: Morning News (1st printing)

99 Poems for the 99 Percent: Morning News (reprint)

The Philadelphia Review of Books blog: By the Waters of Lethe (1st printing)

Poetry: At the End of My Hours, Banana Palace, The Living Teaching, My Sentence, Urgent Care

Poets.org (Poem-A-Day): The Gods Are in the Valley, Watching the Sea Go (1st printing)

Santa Fe Reporter: Moo and Thrall (reprint)

Still Life with Poem: Contemporary Natures Mortes in Verse: By the Waters of Lethe (reprint)

The Volta: En Route

Waxwing: Talk Show

Willow Springs: Melancholia

To Erin Belieu, Jon Davis, Matt Donovan, Louise Glück, Jay Hopler, Carol Moldaw, Kevin Prufer, Peter Streckfus, Arthur Sze, Ann Townsend, and G.C. Waldrep: thanks for lending your eyes to these poems. With enormous gratitude to Michael Wiegers, Tonaya Craft, Kelly Forsythe, Phil Kovacevich, and everyone at Copper Canyon Press, to David Grey (best neighbor in the world), and to my sister, Caryn.

CONTENTS

3   Across the Sea

9   Dmitry Itskov: A Cento

11   The Gods Are in the Valley

13   Morning News

15   Talk Show

16   By the Waters of Lethe

18   Moo and Thrall

21   Lady Xoc

23   Urgent Care

26   A Debris Field of Apocalypticians —
a Murder of Crows

29   En Route

     1   *Morning Drizzle, Chicken Little*

     2   *Office Hours*

     3   *Critique*

     4   *Someone Else's Cake*

     5   *Sixth and Cumae*

     6   *Selfie*

     7   *Happy Hour*

     8   *Going Under*

     9   *A Book before Bed*

     10   *Mon semblable, — mon frère!*

41   Fortune Cookie

42   Banana Palace

47   Murray, My

49   The Living Teaching

52   Meanwhile

55   Melancholia

60   My Sentence

61   The Point of the Needle

63   Watching the Sea Go

65   At the End of My Hours

73   *Notes*

77   *About the Author*

BANANA PALACE

ACROSS THE SEA

We used our texting machines
to look up the definition of *soul*

in the middle of class —
thumb-joints at work

above the stitched paper
of actual books in which

we'd been reading
poetry
       about a Prophetess,

          one of the human cave-bound Time Machines…

She had traveled a long way through the four dimensions
        to be with us.

From someone's mouth to someone's ear.

Someone's hand
        to tablet, papyrus, parchment, paper, the liquid crystal light
        of our computer screens —

Liquid crystal light they'd really
called it that,
        the inventors

        at Marconi Wireless.

"See if you can hear anything,
   Mr. Kemp!" Marconi had cried, the day they sailed the letter *S*

  across the sea—I loved

the synesthesia of that, *See if you can hear,* they'd coaxed some radio waves
   to propel the alphabet
   through the air—

Was that Marconi wishing

he was a liquid crystal light and not a
   break of bones

   that had to fear the future—

      2

A human-headed bird, the Egyptians said.

A butterfly, an *innermost.*

A Web site
   I was afraid to enter: *wewantyoursoul.com* the students
   laughed and laughed—

   soul-adorning, soul-afflicting, soul-amazing—

   soul-and-body-lashings—

They really called it that, the ropes they wound
round oilskin
   to keep out sea and storm, our sailing men—

who sent the cheeriest message you could imagine
to usher in
     the Telegraphic Age: *Thanks*

    am well—

The soul, it was an ellipse in white, it fizzed,
their chaplains said, with God's
     CPR,

       "breath of life"—

So they could travel
      through length and width and depth and time and
      man a ship—

      where someone
      in a small room
         would tap out a message—

      to a far man on a far shore, and they
         would understand one another…

3

He shared all roads and he braved all seas with me,
all threats of the waves and skies is what the Hero says

of his dead father—but it sounded like *soul* to me.

Guide companion—Captain
      of the ship of flesh I had to ride, where "I"

was a third thing in the closed grip
        of the body's vise—

Marconi, he thought he'd hear
        the agony of Christ

        with a sensitive dial to help him sieve.

He trawled
        the frequencies—

        for *eli lama sabachthani* no song lost—

        no impress of tongue and teeth that made a sound, *ever lost*—

        if you had a receiver—

        a virgin say, in a mountain crag, or a brain-bot
                from the tnano-future, did it

                matter which—

                You'd have a house

                for a god's mouth

                and it would message you
                        your rescue...

Rescued from what is what I'm trying to mean.

Rescued from what *you have to fear the future*
        more than you used to which sounded like the soul

        waving a series of flags at me—

4

We wanted arrival to be instant
because we didn't want to be separate
        from what we loved.

Wireless, weightless, and omniscient is how we
refined our machines—

We had a dream

that we could smash the bans
of matter and time and
        still be alive—

Was that the soul, wishing

we would invent the body
out of existence,
        so many of us now

        enthralled by doom...

The students peer so deep into their handheld screens they
        look like Diviners.

Each one
        a scrying Sibyl at the world's

end—
        scribbled-on leaves thrown out of their caves

        and into the wind—

The only part of the Epic
I make them read, just after

      the crew is borne ashore, but before

      the walk amongst the dead—

The part between.

Where there's a body, agonized by light.

      And someone lost.

      And a query—

DMITRY ITSKOV: A CENTO

Dmitry Itskov, 32, has a colossal dream: an early start
    for his own

      mechanical face.

He's one of the men with brains, wondering How—

To evade
    the death of meat, he thinks—

By 2045 we'll have "substance-
    independent minds," then

    no need for biology at all...

At 25, he started to have the symptoms of a midlife crisis:

the musical instruments unlearned, the books unread—

The more he contemplated the world, the more broken it seemed—

"What we're doing here does not look like the behavior of grown-ups,
    killing the planet and killing ourselves."

Decoupling the mind from the needy human body
    could pave the way for a more sublime human spirit—

    It could allow paralyzed people to communicate,
    or control a robotic arm or a wheelchair—

    It could allow you to start your car if you think,
    "Start my car"—

Within a century, we'll frequent "body service shops,"
         choose our bodies from a catalogue, then

              transfer our consciousness
              to one better suited for life on Mars—

"From the very beginning," he said, "we realized Dmitry
         was not an ordinary person."

              He leads a life that could best be described as monastic—

              No meat, fish, coffee, alcohol, or cold water—

              Meat gives him an energy he's "not comfortable with."

What is the brain? What is consciousness?

It contains plenty of terrifying, brink-of-extinction plot twists.

It's somewhere between a cellphone call and teleportation.

It's speaking with his voice in real time.

Get right up close to Dmitry Itskov and sniff all you like—

He has the kind of generically handsome face and perfect smile
         that seem computer generated,

              complete with all the particulars of consciousness and personality—

Yes, we have seen this movie and yes, it always leads to robots
         enslaving humanity—

              For now, just acquiring a lifelike robotic head
              is a splurge.

THE GODS ARE IN THE VALLEY

eighth century, Chinese

The mind sports god-extensions.

It's the mountain from which
    the tributaries spring: self, self, self, self—

      rivering up
            on curling plumes
      from his elaborate
          headpiece

      of smoke.

His head's on fire.

Like a Paleolithic shaman
    working now in the realm of air, he

    folds his hands—

No more casting bones
    for the consulting seeker, this gesture

    seems to mean.
        Your business, his flaming head suggests,

        is with your thought-machine.

How it churns and churns.

Lord Should and Not-Enough,
      Mute the Gigantor, looming dumb

    with her stringy hair —

    Deadalive Mom-'n'-Dad (in the sarcophagus
    of parentheses

    you've placed them) —

He's a yogi, your man
    with a hat of smoke. Serene, chugging out streams

    of constructed air…

Mind's an accident
    of bio-wiring, is one line of thinking.

We're animals that shit out
    consciousness, is another.

The yogi says:
    you must understand yourself

    as projected vapor.
        Thus achieve your

    superpower.

MORNING NEWS

We were mutants, we were being
        put into groups.

Assigned a patch of gymnasium floor—

A gelatinous plasma with star-sparking
        was part of my body—

Next to me a woman who grew food from her skin, we would
        never go hungry—

as I lit our escape
        through tunneling darks.

Which was the beginning of a different, more
        courageous dream—

Self-lit, self-fed, we'd be
        compensating masters for the world's

        want—

        throwing out thread
                so we could grow enormous in oval webs—

Gently led to lie down—

Hard mats on the gymnasium floor and then
        I woke up—

A regular member of the day parade, not
     changed at all —

Despite the speeding heft of the changed life, its
     morning news —

The death of ice, of food, of space, what
     we call Doom —

          which might be a bending —

          a flow of permissions —

          to forge a mutant form —

TALK SHOW

I'm being interviewed on a television talk show, I'm an expert on breathing. "Sooo," the host croons. "Oxygen. How's that feel?" "Like having an alien in your chest," I say, and the live audience roars. "Let's see you breathe," the host says. "Go ahead, lung up—" and I do, inhaling and exhaling to wild applause.

—

It's billed as an "in-depth two-part exclusive" on retaining the use of all my limbs. "Which do you like better," the host asks, "twirling your hair or jiggling your foot? Opening a door or kicking it closed? Which," he leans in, "would you prefer: Parkinson's or polio?" Flustered, I start to stand up and he slaps his hands to his face, saying, "She's standing up, ladies and gentlemen, she's *standing up*—" and I freeze, to mounting applause, half in and half out of my chair.

—

It's another television talk show and I'm "the Doctor of Digestion," a metabolic whiz. They wheel me out to the stage, perched on an old-timey stand-up scale. "Sooo," the host croons. "Food. How's that feel?" Someone cues video and we turn to montage: laparoscopic images of everything I've had to eat for the last three days. "Carne Adovada!" the announcer booms. "Split Pea Soup!" Each announcement meets with wild applause. When the video ends I turn back to the host but find you, smoldering comfortably in the host's appointed chair—you lean forward smiling, your skull-eye gleams, you stick your black-boned finger right down my throat.

BY THE WATERS OF LETHE

      Who will help me avoid my meat
suit?
      Who will help me

      never again, I need an excarnation
specialist —
      Having *been* born,

      I get so tired
waiting and waiting for the world to end —
      Such a slow

      drip,
rushed by occasional
      devastations: flood, fire, storm, plague, the whole

      routine — Still,
we keep arriving, so much meat born
      every day

      amongst the racket of bones: the ice slide, the ocean rise, the wrecks
of megalopoli
      along the coasts — Monster corn. Methane

      glory holes.
Hasn't there been
      enough of that, on the Plain

      of Forgetfulness,
that waste — how many times I've crossed! — of rock and flame.
      These days,

you ghost through that and arrive alive in a world
that burns just the same.

Fuck that. I'm going back to Camp

Oblivion—

MOO AND THRALL

Some people like to be
        spectacularly swayed.

By a red field
        and a glint of metal.

A surgeon's knife. A gun. A pole
        that holds up a banner…

I want to tell you about what I saw,
        on the quad.

Just-dead flesh-babies twelve feet high.

Monkey-head strapped in a test contraption,
        the enormous caption:
IF THIS IS ANIMAL CRUELTY THEN
        —WHAT IS THIS—
Late term.
        They looked like smashed melons. One still latched

        to the cord—

You ask what I thought. I thought,

Who am I to judge
        what another person needs.

Who am I to have to pay
        attention—

I'd wanted coffee and walked into
        a carnival of death.

But death was always
        ho-humming it, in various forms,

        all over the doomèd land—

Still, students clustered.

Young men offered to play the ballast

for the scaffolding
        from which the lurid pictures flared. I thought,

Look at that: something labeled
        "free speech board"—

At either end of the kill-display, where you could
        dig a marker
into white butcher paper— *Get Your Fucking Hands
        Off My Body*—in girlish
curlicue.

Across the quad the clinicians waited.

Across the quad sat the rational young, offering *info*
        on colored paper, it
couldn't compete
        with lunchtime Grand Guignol—

I wanted some coffee.

I wanted some coffee and a sweet croissant.

I wanted and walked
            through the moo and thrall, how hadn't I
seen it—chalked
            underfoot, every few paces the same
smeared message:

            YOU
            ARE
            LOVED

LADY XOC

You're supposed to say *shoke* but I like *shock*.

Lady Shock.

Who drew a spiked rope through her
        offering tongue to
burn blood
        into the threads of bark paper, coax

        a smoke—

        so she could froth up
            the Vision Snake…

Mouths.
        In this particular design

        the Snake has two. The lower

disgorges a warrior-god and the upper the ancestral
        general-king—

Two mouths: you'd think,
        two opposite positions. You'd think she faced

        a breaking choice:

        Do/Don't
        Kill/

            Save—

For wisdom she went to a fanged mouth,
        Lady Shock.

So she could answer
        a trick question: man or god

        of war—

I like
        how honest they were, the old

        tribes.

Look how she kneels
        in tranced adoration, the long spear pointed

        at her brow.

URGENT CARE

Having to make eye contact
        with the economy—

A ball cap that says
        In Dog Years I'm Dead—"The moon

will turn *blood red* and then
        disappear for a while," the TV enthused. Hunched

over an anatomy textbook, a student
        traces a heart

        over another heart—lunar eclipse.

In the bathroom, crayoned
        graffiti:
                fuck the ♥

        —

He collected CAPTCHA, one seat over,
        Mr. feverish *Mange Denied:*

like *puzzling sabbath* or
        street pupas; we shared

some recent typos: *I'm*
        mediated (his), my *tiny bots*

of stimulation, he
        loved the smudged

and swoony words that proved him
      human—

not a machine trying to infiltrate
      the servers

of the *New York Times,* from which he launched
      (*gad shakes* or *hefty lama*)

obits and exposés, some recipes, a digital pic of someone else's
      black disaster, he

lobbed links at both of his fathers (step and bio),
      a few former lovers, a high school coach, a college chum, some people

"from where I used to work," so much info
      (we both agreed), "The umbra,"

the TV explained, shadow
      that Earth was about to make—

—

    …and if during the parenthesis they felt a strange uneasiness…

    …firing rifles and clanging copper pots to rescue the threatened…

    …so benighted and hopelessly lost…

    …their eyes to the errors…

MOON LORE, *Farmers' Almanac.* Waiting room,
      hour two.

—

Urgent Care. That was pretty
        multivalent. As in:

        We really need you to take care of this.
        We really need you

        to care for this.
        To care about this. We really need you

to peer through the clinic's
        storefront window, on alert

        for the ballyhooed moon —

And there it was. Reddening

in its black sock, deep
        in the middle of the hour, of someone's

        nutso-tinsel talk on splendor —

My fevered friend. Describing

the knocked-out flesh. Each of our heads
        fitting like a flash drive

        into the port of a healer's hands.

A DEBRIS FIELD OF APOCALYPTICIANS —
A MURDER OF CROWS

The fact of suffering is not a question of justice.

Belief in God is not a disease.

Our father projections met and disaster ensued.

Earth is our only time machine.

Our mother projections met and disaster ensued.

Everyone is sick from what we made.

He wanted you to ask him how he felt —

he didn't give a shit about your *Umwelt.*

But your heartburn, biome, phone bills, research —

your temperature, heartbreak, dust mites, checkbook —

your live ones, loved ones, languishing spider mums —:

they just needed some shit
                              to make them grow —

The fact of suffering is not a question of justice.

Everyone is sick from what we made.

You watched monks change sand into a Palace of Time,

wheeled through an age of unpardonable crimes.

EN ROUTE

one day, from morning to dream

1 *Morning Drizzle, Chicken Little*

Man in self-argument crossing the street:

"You better wash your mouth out with soap!" "No, *you* better—"

"Umbrellas?"

"Umbrellas?"

"Umbrellas?"

"Umbrellas?"

another man ventured through thickening air—

2 *Office Hours*

You changed your religious affiliation to FOOD

Then: BANDAGES

Then: ORGIAST

        FOXTROT

        ROENTGEN

        TANDOORI

        D played BYLINED *for 72 points!*

        D played CANOODLE *for 96 points!*

        D played ENABLERS *for 65 points!*

   "*Scrabble?*" — student head through the doorway —

        did he think you'd be plotting against carnage —

3 *Critique*

—*mandated*

    interactions with chairs your corporation
      of atoms its forced
mergers
    with air and food was it
      any wonder
    that extending a hand meant "'Tears,'" you said,

      tapping the stanza—"Don't they often
      accompany 'heart'?"

4 *Someone Else's Cake*

She frowned off the sugared flower.

Asked if they'd used butter to beat
      the batter.

Did it suffer from nuts or eggs or fruit?
      She dug her thumb

      into the bother.

5 *Sixth and Cumae*

Some aftermath camped atop a subway grate, some
boxed-'n'-muttering, perpetually
hungry and insane—

"You look like you want me, but you
          don't—" she spat in disgust. "Go make technology happy."

6 *Selfie*

Lips pursed—right index finger
      tipping the chin—the look of

    Um—

7 *Happy Hour*

— a feeling in your body as if you were flinging up
            handfuls of coins—

                    your body rushing back into your arms—

                    •
"I dunno, I wanted it to be more ..." he
                    eddied his fingers, punctuated stars.

8 *Going Under*

"You cannot get ready," her vinyl purse,
       "you cannot get ready for God, you cannot get ready," her stout legs,
         her Sunday-gloved

       grip on the hour —

Shoes black
        patent leather low
          pumps —

tapping, "you cannot get ready," she dug
        into the tunneling train a wide
          berth —

             for blessing you and judging you, how you weren't
               "ready for God" —

       serenely
          deeming you lost —

             You watched her purse swing
               under the East

               River —

…Despite this expense, some epitaphs were resolutely nihilist: "Into nothing from nothing how quickly we go"; while *non fui, fui, non sum, non curo* (I was not, I was, I am not, I don't care) was so common that it was often abbreviated to simply *nffnsnc*…

ttfn —

ta ta for now —

10 *Mon semblable, — mon frère!*

— inexplicable clown wig lurching away with a haul-swing of coats —

FORTUNE COOKIE

You will never get death
out of your system.

BANANA PALACE

I want you to know
how it felt to hold it,
        deep in the well of my eye.

You, future person: star of one of my
complicated dooms—

This one's called Back to the Dark.

Scene 1: Death stampedes through the server-cities.

Somehow we all end up living in caves, foraging in civic ruin.

Banana Palace—the last
        of the last of my kind who can read
        breathes it hot
                into your doom-rimed ear.

She's a dowser of spine-broken books and loose paper
        the rest of your famishing band thinks mad.

                —

Mine was the era
of spending your time
        in town squares made out of air.

You invented a face
        and moved it around, visited briefly
        with other faces.

Thus we streamed
down lit screens

sharing pictures of animals looking ridiculous —

trading portals to shoes, love, songs, news, somebody's latest
        rabid cause: bosses, gluten, bacon, God —

Information about information was the pollen we
deposited —
        while in the real fields bees starved.

        Into this noise sailed
        Banana Palace.

        —

It was a mother ship of gold.

Shining out between HAPPY BDAY KATIE!
        and a photo of someone's broken toe —

Like luminous pillows cocked on a hinge,
like a house
        with a heavy lid, a round house of platelets and honey —

It was open,
        like a box that holds a ring.

        And inside, where the ring would be:

        —

I think about you a lot, future person.

How you will need
all the books that were ever read
        when the screens and wires go dumb.

Whatever you haven't used
        for kindling or bedding.

Whatever made it through
        the fuckcluster of bombs
        we launched accidentally,

        at the end of the era of feeling like no one
        was doing a thing

        about our complicated dooms—

Helpless and braced we sat in dark spaces

submerged in pools of projected images,
        trying to disappear into light—

        Light! There was so much light!
        It was hard to sleep.

        —

Anyway.

Banana Palace.

Even now when I say it, cymbals
        shiver out in spheres. It starts to turn its
        yellow gears

and opens like a clam. Revealing

a fetal curl on its temple floor,
            bagged and sleeping—

a white cocoon

under lit strings that stretch
            from floor to ceiling—

a harp made of glass

incubating
a covered

——

pearl—

We broke the world
you're living in,
            future person.

Maybe
that was always our end:
            to break the jungles to get at the sugar, leave behind
            a waste of cane—

There came a time
I couldn't look at trees without
            feeling elegiac—as if nature

            were already *over,*
                        if you know what I mean.

It was the most glorious thing I had ever seen.

Cross section of a banana under a microscope
the caption read.

I hunched around my little screen
sharing a fruit no one could eat.

MURRAY, MY

FEED ME
            caterwauler — a meat-sack
with another meat-sack for a pet, I
            tended hunger — his and mine, the baby moles
he'd bat to death, the low-slung
            hunt near the sink
for chicken grease — my
            teacher-beast — he liked it

raw or cooked or canned or kibbled, he'd
            clip a claw to my lower lip
if I was asleep — so that I'd
            pad to the kitchen and slop his bowl
with *seafood medley* or *chicken-beef,* I'd
            grab him up — squeeze so tight I thought I'd
pop, croon
            silly silly silly silly and watch his eyes
close down to slits, I

            tended hunger — it was on my mind a lot
as I watched the climate curl and bang, were you
            watching too? Wondering if you'd
hesitate to eat your cat
            in the new extreme
of flood and flame, I had a brute
            hypochondria
about the future's body — all around me

summer burst its sack of seeds
in trumpet horns of purple-blue I loved
　　so much I cut them once
to bring inside—where they
　　promptly died—and thus
I knew—no matter how much
　　I loved the world, to hunger
was to be
　　a destroyer—

THE LIVING TEACHING

You wanted to be a butcher
but they made you be a lawyer.

You brought home presents
when it was nobody's birthday.

Smashed platters of meat
she cut against the grain.

Were a kind
      of portable shrine —

          I was supposed to cultivate a field of bliss,
          then return to my ordinary mind.

You burned the files
and moved the office.

Made your children fear
a different school.

Liked your butter hard
and your candy frozen.

Were a kind
      of diamond drill, drilling a hole
      right through my skull —

      quality sleep, late November.

What did it mean, "field of bliss" —

A sky alive "with your greatest mentor" —

I wore your shoes, big as boats,
                flopped through the house —

                while you made garlic eggs with garlic salt, what

                "represents the living teaching" —

Sausages on toasted rye with a pickle,
and a smother of cheese, and
frosting
                right out of the can without the cake —

You ruled
                with a knife in one hand and a fork in the other, you raged
                at my stony mother, while I banged

                from my high chair, waving
                the bloodied bone

                of something slaughtered — I was
                a butcher's daughter.

So all hail to me —

                Os Gurges, Vortex Mouth, I gap my craw
                and the bakeries of the cities fall, I

                stomp the docks — spew out a bullet-stream
                of oyster shells, I'll

drain the seas — the silos
on every farm, the rice

from the paddy fields, the fruit
from all the orchard trees, and then I'll

eat the trees —

I'll eat with money and I'll eat
with my teeth until the rocks

and the mountains curl
and my blood sings —

I'm such a good girl

to eat the world.

MEANWHILE

She had a parched heart, *Araneus illaudatus.*

She had a name
        in her own tongue, wasn't
a Roman Senator, wasn't
          orb-weaver

        with a rocking chair and corncob pipe—

What
        could true her name, she was

        wholly alien—

A fanged knob, body
        big as my thumb—

        to the first joint.

        —

Poised for hours in her spun palace her
        deeply unreadable mind—

She drained the night-moths.

She'd disappear for a day or two,
        turn up bigger than before—

Blood-pumped
        until she split her seams, pulsed out
from her old skin,
        flexing like a fist—

Illaudatus:
      unpraised.

—

Did I not wed her, did I not worship—

Handfast
      to her twilight appearance

every evening in summer—
      When she dropped to head-level I crawled

      into the lit house—

Sat up
      just inside the door, adrenalined,

—

      afraid—

Autumn came and the web sagged.

Winter came with its pit mouth
      and I stayed inside.

Now it's spring and her eggs have hatched
      in the crook of the deck chair—babies

      getting ready to balloon—

Soon they'll hook the wind and
      web up

in someone's eaves, thimbles
          of blood and bite

                    —

          at the center of the weave—

They'd fanned out over the canvas seat, they had
          a penchant for spinning.

A drive for blood and a drive to be, which is
          everyone's condition…

I took a thin box and made one side a shuttle.
          Started to airlift

          the orange tribe—

but made an orange smear. And so I smeared them all,
          her children.

MELANCHOLIA

1

Dad and I on a summer motorcycle ride; I'm eleven. It's incredibly hot, already, as we exit the pancake house. I long to ride without my helmet: how cool it will feel, how I will have to close my eyes against the rush — Just then Dad says, "Should we wear our helmets?"

2

It's the kind of movie where a rogue planet named Melancholia is bearing down on Earth, but someone's getting married — she's very depressed. At the reception her boss won't stop hounding her to write better ad copy; her mother insults her while giving a toast. Unsurprisingly, she keeps trying to leave her own wedding: once to fuck a coworker, once, incredibly, to take a long bath. People keep trying to change other people's feelings. They cite "real scientists" and the broadcast schematics: "They say Melancholia will just pass us by!"

3

Lying in effigy on the couch in the family room, home from work early and not saying a word — after days he'd get up and it'd be a party.

4

The first time I saw a picture of King Henry VIII, I couldn't believe he had been my dad. *Star Trek*'s Captain Kirk, actor Brian Keith — one the blowhard Commander rake of space, the other as a diver with a laudanum addiction, sinking in a sea of hallucination as the Krakatoa volcano explodes.

5

Sometimes you meet your secret suicidal death wish with bravado and buy a brand new Datsun 280Z. When your wife goes out of town you promise your nine-year-old daughter you'll take her to dinner and you do, strapping your bodies into your rocket ship. You're about to turn left from the cul-de-sac where you live, when a car careens around the corner and nearly hits you. Enraged, you follow it to a driveway, and when it's parked you get out, demanding the teenage driver pay you some mind.

6

As if I'd known—not thirty minutes later, bike sliding out from us, taking the gravel in the curve. I blacked out for the bulk of it, but for the sudden apparitions, rushing round-mouthed from an old green car—then I was on the bike again and we were gunning the highway: Dad would have to have his broken shoulder set. In the hospital waiting room I hefted my helmet, turning it around, tracing the deep score and the drag—

7

"Yeah," I say. "We should wear our helmets."

8

Meanwhile, Melancholia approaches. You stop paying your taxes and soon, without telling her, you stop paying your wife's. You stockpile Leicas and stereo equipment; you bring home a big telescope we only use twice. You're about to die soon and you want it all for you. You're about to die soon because you have just turned fifty and you know you can never outlive your father: fifty-four years old when he was brained by a tumor. Sometimes it seems like you've quit going to work. Sometimes it seems like you're a traumatized Hansel, stashing candy in bags in a closet. And regarding those taxes: everyone said your father was a saint, but you always knew he was a secret gambler — you've banked on the moon that blew up in his head.

9

What is a father, what is a star? Fathers blaze glorious at the edge of home planets, they explode above islands and boil the sea. Fathers blast in and flatten the forests: you're amazed, in the photographs, how many miles of trees.

10

In the dream, the royal family has died. Like all subjects, I'm being ushered into a room where I am to pick liquors from a cabinet: thus we submit to the annihilation of the king and his line. I am careful about what and how much I choose, because I am the father of an ordinary family, and I am deeply unsettled by the death of kings. I want to get out from under the eye of the cabinet functionaries, who stand watchful in their fur-lined cloaks — they flank the cabinet, which is portable and gilded like an altar. I choose two Malt 40s for myself, because those are the spirits of the father; mothers receive liquors more delicate. I'm unnerved by the ceremony, by my own

curled-toed shoes —

II

Meanwhile, your daughter's trapped inside your rocket ship. She's fixed at the window, watching your rage, so private and familiar, batter a stranger. You ram into the kid and he rams you back, until you topple over— then he jumps on your chest and flails at your face. Finally his own dad comes out and pulls the boy off you. He says, "Go home—" pointing his finger just like you're a dog. And when you get back in the car, exuberant, bloodied, breathing hard—

12

Fathers get angry if you leave open the screen door or sell weapons to Syria, if you ask for some juice but only drink half. If the sprinklers soak through the morning paper, if there are too many leftovers in the fridge in foil—how then can the fathers target the drones? Use the wrong knife on a prime cut of meat and they'll set off the end of the world.

13

After the dinner you put on your coats and return to Dad's rocket ship. He's going to keep flying as if no one is shipwrecked, he's going to step on the gas of his disintegrating car—"Let's drive fast!" you cry and he says, "What road?" It's a thrill to accelerate and fly through the night. It really feels as if you could go up and up, punching through clouds until you hurtle free into the whisk of stars—he slams on the brakes. It's been raining for days in your birthday desert, and there's a flood raging across the road. A giant tractor tire bobs by and sinks in the roil. You climb out of the car and stand next to your father, who says, "Look at that—" enthralled

by the surging water—

14

I wake up and decide the dream is stupid. I spend all day not writing it down. "But look," my sister says, when I later tell her about it. "You chose the spirit of the father."

MY SENTENCE

 —spring wind with its
    train of spoons,
kidney-bean-shaped
    pools, Floridian
humus, cicadas with their
    electric appliance hum, cricket
pulse of dusk under
    the pixilate gold of the trees, fall's
finish, snow's white
    afterlife, death's breath
finishing the monologue Phenomena, The Most Beautiful Girl *you*
    carved the word because you craved the world—

THE POINT OF THE NEEDLE

Since you got to behead
each
        hollyhock crown

        with your round
        guillotine

        of a mouth —

I hope you get to spin inside your
        paper house.

        Emerge Noctuidae,
        owlet moth,

        laying your eggs in leaves at night.

That you might finish your stitch —

Replicate yourself in time so you are
        always present —

        each egg a deposit —

        an echo-pearl of "you" along time's string —

That my soul might be allowed
        to flourish —

Make a success
        of threading flesh, to participate

again in time, on

long arcs between sets of plunge, even though
       it hurt—

       to be born and die—

       it loved to ride
             the point

             of the needle—

WATCHING THE SEA GO

Thirty seconds of yellow lichen.

Thirty seconds of coil and surge,
       fern and froth, thirty seconds
              of salt, rock, fog, spray.

                            Clouds
moving slowly to the left —

       A door in a rock through which you could see

              ——

another rock,
       laved by the weedy tide.

       Like filming breathing — thirty seconds

of tidal drag, fingering
       the smaller stones
              down the black beach — what color

       was that, aquamarine?
Starfish spread

       their salmon-colored hands.

              ——

I stood and I shot them.

I stood and I watched them
   right after I shot them: thirty seconds of smashed sea
    while the real sea

    thrashed and heaved—

They were the most boring movies ever made.
I wanted

    to mount them together and press Play.

     —

   Thirty seconds of waves colliding.
Kelp

   with its open attitudes, seals
    riding the swells, curved in a row

    just under the water—

     the sea,
over and over.
     Before it's over.

AT THE END OF MY HOURS

I

here I'm here I'm here I'm

here here here here cricket

pulse — the katydidic *tick*

(and then a pause) *tick*

(and then a pause) in greening trees — tales

of a gratitude for water, the hollyhock's

trumpet *Yes,* Tenderness

her glove and hoe — her bad trip

love/grief, her medic tent

talking me down, kissed fissures

in the world's despair, what I'd

loved — alive for a while — a day called

Rip and Brood, a day called

Glorious Hour, the long hunt and the worm found

in the battered petunias — every

morning in summer

that last summer

before the bees collapsed and the seas rose up

to say *Fuck You*

2

perplexed by how it hadn't been

unfailingly compatible, our

being numerous — how half the time

we couldn't see the shapes

we were supposed to make

made grave our disasters — a god's glass

bearing down

to burn the wheat crop — to keep time alive

inside a tomato, splicing

fish into fruit — some

wanted to defy limitation

were offered famine

bric-a-brac townships

virtual cities

where you could stand in market aisles

still expecting cherries

3

his rhythms were your rhythms

Murray the cat—sleeping à deux

draped your length from hip to knee

like a scabbard—unsheathed his yawn

tortured finches for breakfast

yowled and yowled round the ravaged bowl

till you fed him chicken

from your own plate

another mouth

pearling the wheel of appetite, coveting

a bloody mash

to keep it going—such a dumb rondeau

who invented it!

eating to live to kill to eat, even

cat on a stick when fields failed, no

crave for rain against the blasted scape

nor love nor god at the end

of my hours, but

garlic and butter

a splash of cognac

steak frites

4

and when soil burned and order failed

and dogs then people starved in char I remembered

an extraordinary peace, the privilege

of being left alone with bread to eat

and famous butter "the chefs use," the venues

of white sleep, cannabis and Klonopin

the soma-goods of art and when

my back went up against a blackened wall

for rumored beans in dented cans I forgot

my body—became a future remembering

how it got that way, some

blah blah blah—about hoarding rivers

and hiding gold, we

died in droves—we killed each other and we

killed ourselves until our bones wore out

their plastic shrouds

5

I couldn't quite

quit some ideas — trees and chocolate

I couldn't stop yammering

over devastated Earth

pining for nachos — prescription drugs

and a hint of spring, though I could see

the new desert — its bumper crop

of bone and brick

from shipwrecked cities — where now

the sons and daughters of someone tough

are on the hunt for rat — the scent of meat

however mean and a root

sending an antenna up, to consider

greening — what poems built their houses for

once, in a blindered age, teaching us

the forms we felt, in rescue — hoarded-up scraps

whirling around my cave

trying to conjure peaches

NOTES

Across the Sea

1   Guglielmo Marconi pioneered the development of long-distance radio transmission. Details in the poem of his activities come from "Marconi's Achievement: Telegraphing Across the Ocean without Wires" (*McClure's Magazine,* February 1902). Toward the end of his life, Marconi literally dreamed of inventing a device that could pick up any sounds made at any time in the past—a dream based on the mistaken conviction that sound waves never die.

3   "He shared all roads and he braved all seas with me, / all threats of the waves and skies": Book VI, *The Aeneid;* translated from the Latin by Robert Fagles (2006).

"*Eli lama sabachthani*": Christ's plea on the cross: "My God, why have you forsaken me?"

4   "The only part of the Epic / I make them read" being Book VI of *The Aeneid,* wherein hero Aeneas visits the cave-bound prophetess, the Sibyl of Cumae, to ask his fortune and speak to the shade of his dead father. The Sibyl was infamous for scribbling her prophecies on oak leaves and leaving them to the wind to scatter, for hapless seekers to try to catch.

Dmitry Itskov: A Cento

All but lines 4–6 are text rearranged or verbatim from: Bianca Bosker, "Dmitry Itskov Knows He'll Live Forever," *Huffington Post,* June 18, 2013; and David Segal, "This Man Is Not a Cyborg. Yet," *New York Times,* June 1, 2013.

The Gods Are in the Valley

This poem was sparked by an illustration in *The Secret of the Golden Flower*, attributed to Lü Yen, eighth century. Translated from the Chinese by Richard Wilhelm (1931).

By the Waters of Lethe

In the Greek bardo, shades of the dead were required to drink from the River Lethe in order to forget their earthly life. Only then would they march toward reincarnation.

Lady Xoc

Lady Xoc was one of the most powerful women in Maya civilization. She is famously depicted on the lintels of carved doorways at Yaxchilan, an eighth-century Maya city in what is now Chiapas, Mexico. For more, read Dennis Tedlock's excellent *2000 Years of Mayan Literature* (2011).

Urgent Care

A CAPTCHA is a type of challenge-response test used in computing to determine whether a user is human. One common CAPTCHA requires that the user type in the letters of a distorted word or phrase presented on-screen.

A Debris Field of Apocalypticians — a Murder of Crows

Umwelt (German): environment; also "self-centered world" (semiotics); also "being-in-the-world" (Gestalt psychology).

En Route

Sixth and Cumae
"…out of the rocky flanks of Cumae… an enormous cavern pierced by a hundred tunnels, / a hundred mouths with as many voices rushing out, / the Sibyl's rapt replies": Book VI, *The Aeneid;* translated from the Latin by Robert Fagles (2006).

A Book before Bed
The passage between ellipses comes from Jerry Toner's *Popular Culture in Ancient Rome* (2009).

Mon semblable, — mon frère!
"My likeness, my brother!" (Baudelaire, by way of Eliot).

The Living Teaching

The phrases in quotation marks come from Robert Thurman's talk on refuge field meditation in *Circling the Sacred Mountain* (1999). Refuge field meditation begins with visualizing and invoking your primary spiritual mentor to accompany you on the path to enlightenment.

Melancholia

This poem refers to two movies: *Melancholia,* a 2011 arthouse apocalypse by Lars von Trier, and *Krakatoa, East of Java,* a 1969 disaster flick.

Dana Levin's first book, *In the Surgical Theatre,* was chosen by Louise Glück for the 1999 American Poetry Review/Honickman First Book Prize. Copper Canyon Press brought out her second book, *Wedding Day,* in 2005, and in 2011 her third, *Sky Burial,* which the *New Yorker* called "utterly her own and utterly riveting." *Sky Burial* was noted for 2011 year-end honors by the *New Yorker,* the *San Francisco Chronicle, Coldfront,* and *Library Journal.*

Levin's poetry and essays have appeared in many anthologies and magazines, including *The Best American Poetry 2015,* the *New York Times, Los Angeles Review of Books, Boston Review,* the *American Poetry Review, Poetry* magazine, and the *Paris Review.* Her fellowships and awards include those from the National Endowment for the Arts, PEN, the Witter Bynner Foundation, and the Library of Congress, as well as the Rona Jaffe, Whiting, and Guggenheim Foundations.

A teacher of poetry for over twenty years, Levin serves as Distinguished Writer-in-Residence at Maryville University, Saint Louis, where she teaches every fall. She lives in Santa Fe, New Mexico.

Poetry is vital to language and living. Since 1972, Copper Canyon Press has published extraordinary poetry from around the world to engage the imaginations and intellects of readers, writers, booksellers, librarians, teachers, students, and donors.

WE ARE GRATEFUL FOR THE MAJOR SUPPORT PROVIDED BY:

THE PAUL G. ALLEN
FAMILY FOUNDATION

TO LEARN MORE ABOUT UNDERWRITING
COPPER CANYON PRESS TITLES,
PLEASE CALL 360-385-4925 EXT. 103

WE ARE GRATEFUL FOR THE MAJOR SUPPORT PROVIDED BY:

Anonymous

Donna and Matt Bellew

Diana Broze

Janet and Les Cox

Beroz Ferrell & The Point, LLC

Mimi Gardner Gates

Linda Gerrard and Walter Parsons

Gull Industries, Inc.
   on behalf of William and
   Ruth True

Mark Hamilton and Suzie Rapp

Steven Myron Holl

Lakeside Industries, Inc.
   on behalf of Jeanne Marie Lee

Maureen Lee and Mark Busto

Rhoady Lee and Alan Gartenhaus

Ellie Mathews and Carl Youngmann
   as The North Press

John Phillips and Anne O'Donnell

Joseph C. Roberts

Cynthia Lovelace Sears and
   Frank Buxton

The Seattle Foundation

Kim and Jeff Seely

David and Catherine Eaton Skinner

Dan Waggoner

C.D. Wright and Forrest Gander

Charles and Barbara Wright

The dedicated interns
   and faithful volunteers of
   Copper Canyon Press

The Chinese character for poetry is made up of two parts:
"word" and "temple." It also serves as pressmark for
Copper Canyon Press.

The poems are set in Adobe Garamond. Headings are set in
Berthold Akzidenz-Grotesk.
Printed on archival-quality paper.
Book design and composition by Phil Kovacevich.